A MONEY SAVING MINDSET

40 Ways to Help You Save

By Derek L. Polen

Scripture taken from the HOLY BIBLE, NEW INTERNATIONAL VERSION®. Copyright © 1973, 1978, 1984 by International Bible Society. Used by permission of Zondervan Publishing House. All rights reserved.

The New International Version trademark is registered in the United States Patent and Trademark Office by International Bible Society. Use of this trademark requires the permission of International Bible Society

ISBN -13: 978-1497471696   ISBN-10: 1497471699
Printed by Createspace, An Amazon.com Company

To my wife, my best friend

To my children, my inspiration

To everyone who works so hard to provide for their family
and are looking for more ways to save money.

TABLE OF CONTENTS

THE MONEY SAVING JOURNEY

Thank you for purchasing this book. I hope you will benefit greatly from the ideas shared in this book and that you enjoy it as much as I enjoyed creating it for you. As you will see, this book is designed to be a short and simple read, but within the pages ahead there are ideas that can effectively help you change the way you think about saving money. With a little effort and a solid game plan, you will see how easy it is to start saving money and achieving your financial goals.

Over the past 15 years, I have saved thousands of dollars based on various buying strategies, saving ideas, and simple lessons I have learned. Most of these ideas I am about to share with you come from experiences and discoveries I have had throughout my life when I was trying to save the money I worked so hard for, so I could provide a comfortable lifestyle for my family.

Let's face it, today's world is scary. You could lose your job, unexpected expenses occur, and the cost of living continues to rise at a faster rate than our compensation growth. There are two primary reasons why I decided to pursue the journey of writing this book.

Let me share the first reason, an alarming United States Census Bureau (www.census.gov) statistic in their 2012 Poverty Highlights Report:

The official poverty rate in 2012 was 15.0%, which represented 46.5 million people

The number of people in poverty continues to remain near the largest number in the 50+ years of published poverty estimates, based on the U.S. Census Bureau's 2010 report when the record level high was reached. This statistic shows that 15% of the people in America are struggling financially per the "poverty" definition. While that number is heartbreaking, we all know others who are part of the other 85% that struggle with their finances too and are living paycheck to paycheck.

The other reason that tugged on my heart to do this book was from a research study I did. Over the past year I reviewed prayer request submissions from all over the world, but mostly from the United States. Out of all the results, the #1 prayer need was people seeking financial help, primarily paying their bills.

My goal in this book is to help you save as much as you can by sharing with you 40 ways to save. I know you cannot implement all of these ideas, and some do not apply to you. If you can follow through on just a few of these ideas you are on the path of becoming a more cost-conscious consumer.

Stop for a moment and think of ways you could use your savings. Do you have any financial goals? The savings you achieve can help you on a car payment, get ahead on a home mortgage, apply towards college tuition, allow you to quit a part time job, or use to obtain another personal goal. The bottom line is that we can all find ways to help relieve financial burdens and achieve financial goals with the money we can save.

The ideas in this book are listed in four different categories. First, there is the *Shopping Strategy* category, which is comprised of ideas for in-store, online, and product specific savings ideas. These are the easy ones! Then, there is the *Mindset Makers* category with a variety of ways to get you thinking differently, including ideas that can be incorporated on a consistent basis. The next group is

Choices That Save which applies to more specific areas and may consist of harder choices, investments that lead to savings, or apply to the financing side of things. Lastly, *Promotions and Programs* covers the built in benefits that come with many purchases or from retailers.

I developed this guide in an easy, understandable format to give you the general idea for a savings technique. These ideas I am sharing with you will also help you generate other ways to save as it applies to your life. The opportunities to save money are limitless. This guide will give you a solid foundation to start changing your mindset to always think "How can I save money?".

At the end of this book is the Money Saving Game Plan. Some of the strategies I will share can be implemented immediately. There are also strategies that will take time or may not be applicable yet. The Money Saving Game Plan is a consolidated list of all the strategies to help guide you. This small bonus is a simple tool to help you prioritize which ideas to target first, identify which ones are successful or not, track your estimated savings, and record the ways you could generate savings with each idea.

Before we get started on your money saving journey, let me share with you why I chose 40 ways to save.

THE REASON
FOR 40 WAYS

The number 40 has significant meaning in our history. Its importance comes from the Bible showing times of testing that led to reward or fulfillment.

- It rained 40 days/nights causing the flood in Noah's story (Genesis 7:12)
- Moses was on Mount Sinai for 40 days/ nights fasting while receiving the Ten Commandments (Exodus 34:28)
- Elijah's 40 day/night fasting and journey to the mountain of God (1 Kings 19:8)
- Jesus fasted for 40 days and 40 nights (Matthew 4:2)
- After Jesus' resurrection he was on Earth 40 days (Acts 1:3)

This book is an easy read guide with 40 ways to help you save. This approach is about respecting the significance of 40 from our history. Plus, 40 money saving strategies are not too overwhelming, yet substantial enough to give you targets for cost savings, and to help instill a money saving mindset.

SHOPPING STRATEGIES

1. Online Shopping

When buying something online, you must make sure you look for a coupon code (or discount or promotion code) before you complete the transaction. Coupon codes are very fast and simple to find. Right before you enter your payment information in the online checkout, look for a box that says something like "Coupon code" or "Promotion Code". They can save you 10-30% on your purchase.

There are three ways to get coupon codes:

- E-mail - If you are a member of a store's loyalty program or on their mailing list, many stores periodically e-mail coupon codes.

- Catalogs or magazines - Some will have an insert that contains a code. Many advertisements throughout magazines contain savings codes as well.

- Internet - There are two ways I go about searching for coupon codes online. You can go out to any search engine and type in the company name and words "coupon code" after it. There will be several sites pull up. You have to search through and it may take a few tries. In addition to a search engine approach, I go to reliable websites that are good at having up to date coupon codes. Some of those sites are www.upromise.com, www.retailmenot.com, and www.couponmountain.com.

If you are lucky, some stores allow customers to apply 2 or 3 codes per order. When you use a coupon code your savings can range from 10-30% of your order amount, you could get free shipping, or a free gift. For just a couple minutes of work it can yield sizeable savings.

2. Leverage the Competition

With the marketplace becoming more and more competitive many companies offer price matching if you find a lower price from a competitor. If you prefer to shop at a particular store due to location, service, or loyalty program and find their competitor has something you want at a lower price than your store offers, just show them the ad and ask if they will match it.

We see it all the time, price match guarantees on commercials. These usually occur in big box retailers, but you can also apply this same technique to other expenses. Be honest and make sure you are prepared to show the ad or quote of the better priced store.

One highly competitive area that has a high success rate on an expensive item is with tires. When shopping for tires narrow it down to the tire you want. Get quotes from each dealer who sells that tire. If the dealer you prefer because of service is higher priced, show them a quote from another dealer and they will most likely match it. This allows you to win in both areas of pricing and preferred service.

Another example of using competition is using an online competitor in an actual store. I purchased a new cell phone at a big box retailer and needed a new case. The case I wanted was $40. I looked online and found it for $22. They matched the price and I was able to get the case immediately instead of having to wait for it with an online purchase.

Many companies even give you an extra discount on the difference. That additional savings could be another 5-10% on the difference in the two prices. Price matching not only works in retail stores, but can be effective in other shopping outlets such as auto repair shops, car dealerships, or with hotels.

3. In-Store Coupons

Some people are embarrassed to use coupons. Are you embarrassed to save money? I sure am not and it only proves that you are a wise shopper. Who does not like free money? It is like putting money in your bank. Coupons are making a comeback and are extremely worth your time to search for. Newspapers are the most recognized source for obtaining coupons. I sometimes purchase an extra Sunday paper if it is a good coupon week. It costs only $2, but if I can get $10-$100 worth of extra coupons it is worth it. You can also find valuable coupons in magazines, flyers, and phonebooks (yes the latter still exists).

With the internet you can print some coupons from the web. Some manufacturer sites have coupons for individual items and some store sites have coupons that allow you to take a percentage off an item or an entire order. Auto repair chains are other good sites that may have coupons for expensive services such as brake repair or engine maintenance. If a coupon is not available to print, you can sign up on their mailing list and they may send you money saving coupons in the future.

Have you ever bought something and later found a coupon for it? It is so frustrating. Well, some stores actually let you come back in and they will make the adjustment. You have to bring your receipt and the coupon. My wife recently bought a pack-n-play for a baby shower and it cost $220. She ordered online and I went to the store to pick it up. On the counter they had 20% off coupons starting the following week. I mentioned to the employee how I wish my wife waited a week to buy it and she told me just to come back and they would make the adjustment. I saved $46, by noticing the coupon, saying something, and making a quick trip back for savings.

4. Do Your Research

With any big purchase you should always do some research. You want to make sure you get the best value you can, while ensuring you get all the features in the product that you desire. Researching can prevent you from buying the wrong product that you would need to return or from buying a poor quality product that will create more costs in repair or replacement.

You can research many ways:

- Magazines – there are various product review magazines to choose from depending on the item
- Personal Reviews – ask people you know who may have bought the same product
- Online – you can look for random articles, but I prefer the different store sites and there are usually feedback forums on those products with ratings as well. If it is a technology product, Cnet.com is a good source.

5. Buying Clothes

When it comes to wearing clothes, I do like to wear name brand clothes. I never pay full price for these name brands and you do not have to either. There are five ways I can get my shirts that retail for $50 for only $15 or less.

- Shop at Marshalls or T.J. Maxx®. These retailers buy last season, off season, and overstocked merchandise from the designers. You can save up to 70% off the MSRP. To find a location visit: www.tjmaxx.com or www.marshallsonline.com.

- Outlet Malls. The bargains are not as good as they used to be, but you can still find nice items for savings of 50% or more. Some of the best outlet malls are Premium Outlets (www.premiumoutlets.com); and Tanger Outlets (www.tangeroutlet.com).

- Check out the clearance racks at department stores

- Stock up on off season deals

- Use coupons

Mall department stores are a great example of where I can score big by combining the last three ways. You can find nice items that are about out of season in their clearance racks and some offer coupons which could save you a total up to 75% off. Just do not forget what you bought next season!

6. Off Season Values

Do you have extra space to store items? Then save (and store) away with this plan. All you have to do is take that day after Christmas savings mindset to your shopping approach all year round. Here is a list of items to keep in mind for end of season values:

All Year Round
- Holiday merchandise - decorations, supplies, gifts
- Clothing
- Sports equipment – gloves, balls, shoes

End of Summer
- Lawn & Garden – patio furniture, mowers, hoses, tools
- Swim gear
- Outdoor toys
- Fans
- Window or floor air conditioners

End of Winter

- Snow removal tools
- Heaters
- Do-it-yourself insulation kits

This idea does tie up your cash since you are investing for the following year, but it can be worth the investment. If you time it right, stores will start reducing prices about a month before the season close and you can net savings of 50%-70%.

7. Dollar Store Values

One of the funny things my dad always tells my kids when going into a dollar store is "The sky's the limit", meaning they can get whatever they want. If you have not been in a dollar-type store for some time you should check them out now. Some of these stores have everything for $1. Now you will not knock it out of the park with every purchase, but you can get just as good a product for a better price than you would at a big retailer.

I think these stores are great for a variety of things.

- Cleaning supplies
- Gift bags and decorations
- Envelopes
- Containers
- Batteries (watch size only)
- Toothbrushes
- Goody bag treats
- Books, kids activity books, some toys

Be cautious with some foods (check expiration dates), medicines, and cosmetics.

8. Review Your Receipts

When it comes to shopping we tend to trust the accuracy of how much we were charged. Unfortunately though, I catch mistakes on bills all the time. You get charged for something you did not order, an item was duplicated, or a sale price was not rung up correctly.

We moved recently and I noticed our new cable bill was much higher than they quoted at time of setup. I called them and went over my questions. They ended up duplicating a couple things and overcharging on another item, to where it ended up being over $60 more.

I recently took my wife's car in to get some work done. There were several preventive maintenance things they suggested to do. On most of them I declined their service since I knew I could take care of it. When I got the bill I noticed they flushed the radiator. I asked the service manager if they did this and he said yes. I explained that I never approved that and he agreed. He went and adjusted the bill, reducing it by $56. If I did not review my receipt or ask, I would have spent more than I should have.

We have to make sure we take the time to review our receipts for accuracy. It only takes a few seconds to do and a little attention to detail. Do not be afraid to ask the store or customer service rep if you do not understand why you were charged something. Review your receipt, speak up, and do not let yourself get overcharged!

9. Buying A Used Car

All my life I have owned used cars. Used cars are always cheaper and knowing how quickly a new car depreciates, why would you buy new, right? I have to admit I caved and bought a new van after our second child was born. My wife really wanted it and I wanted to make her happy. About a year later, we traded in for a used SUV. I lost a few dollars on that transaction.

I think it is fun to car shop, but it can be intimidating and overwhelming with all the choices out there. It is such a huge purchase and it is normal to stress out about it. If you have done your research you will be fine.

This purchase will be one of the biggest purchases you will make, so you must be prepared. There is plenty of advice out there, but let me share my tips:

- Review a Third Party Car Evaluation. I always require the dealer provide this to me which saves you money from getting your own. Review it thoroughly to make sure there are no records of an accident. If it has been and you are ok with that, then you have documentation to leverage the price down.

- Review Consumer Reports. They have reviews on used cars going back several years and this gives you an idea of the Reliability Ratings of the car you are looking at. This will help you project any potential repairs you may have to make in the future. www.consumerreports.org

- When negotiating, try to squeeze out any extras you can. It could be oil changes, clear coat protection, extra warranty, accessories, and more.

- Do not be afraid to point out items that are missing, broke, or aesthetically displeasing. I do not mean point out every little scratch, but focus on the deal breaker items. I pointed out 2 issues on the upholstery and they knocked off $100, so I would not require them to repair. If you are missing accessories and they have a similar make and model for sale, they are usually good about giving you what is missing or ordering it for you.

MINDSET MAKERS

10. Negotiate!

My parents always said, "It never hurts to ask. The worse thing they can say is no." They are absolutely right. Negotiating is something so many people are afraid to try or do not realize is allowed in a purchase transaction. Unfortunately, many people do not make any attempts to negotiate and leave money or free items on the table.

- If you see a product flaw, ask the manager for a discount. They most likely will give you one because they want it off the shelf and out of their inventory as bad as you want that discount.

- If you are buying in large quantities ask for a discount. Leverage volume!

- Ask for a discount if you pay in cash. This can save you hundreds of dollars. More on this topic later.

- If the only available stock of an item is the display item, ask for discount or suggest a price to the manager you would be willing to pay for the display item.

- At hotels, when you check-in ask for complimentary room upgrades or services. I have received room upgrades to suites or preferred views that were as much as $200 more per night for free, and also got free meals.

- Ask for extras. When we bought that new car I had them throw in a $900 interior/exterior coating protection. Some dealers will give you gift certificates to a restaurant if you ask. If you see smaller items that compliment your purchase just ask them to throw it in before you agree to buy. You will be amazed of how willing places are to throw something in (which is of minimal cost to them) just to close the sale.

11. Reuse / Repurpose

Before you throw something in the trash ask yourself if there is another way you can use that item. It is always frustrating when you have to buy something and you realize that you just threw away something that could have worked. Over the past 6 years I have become a recycling fanatic after studying the environmental impact of what we all throw in the trash. Reusing an item is another way to help keep our environment safer and cleaner.

Here are some examples:

- Old t-shirts = cleaning towels
- Cardboard boxes you receive goods in can be reused to ship items back out.
- Plastic grocery bags = trash can liners
- Old rugs = vehicle trunk/cargo liners
- Gift bags take up little space and you can reuse them for someone else's gift.
- Plastic food containers = storage containers for crayons, nuts and bolts, toys, and more.

There are thousands of ways to reuse something for a different purpose. Another thing we do with kids in school is have a couple drawers of miscellaneous project items. These are items we did not use or already used for something else and cleaned them up. It always seems that when one of our children has a project to do we are scrambling to come up with items to make or decorate the project. Having a couple small drawers dedicated to these tasks helps save us time, money, and allows us to be proactive versus waiting until the last minute to scour the house.

I am NOT suggesting you hoard every little non-waste item for a potential future purpose, but see if you can utilize that item for another purpose so you can prevent spending more money in the future.

12. A Fresh Coat Of Savings

Sometimes all you need is a fresh coat of paint and it makes a world of difference. Before you invest in new drawer and cabinet hardware, which is expensive, try painting what you have. My wife did that on some cabinet knobs and saved us about $70. I did that on some bathroom fixtures and saved about $50.

Another way to save is by buying that paintable item (usually furniture) at a consignment shop or at a garage sale. These items can save you hundreds from buying brand new. The only downside is you have to be patient or more accepting of what is available as you will not get to pick out your style as easily.

Painting a table or other piece of furniture before you replace it can also clean up the look and add a few more years of life to those items. It is very easy to replace something after it looks older, has scratches, or does not match. With a little bit of paint and some Picasso-like skills you can save money and delay expenses.

13. Get Reimbursed

A few years ago I noticed our water bill was enormously high for a couple months. There were no visible leaks in the house, no toilets running, no water in the yard, and the meter was fine. I then went under the house and heard a hissing sound. A water pipe on the ground had a small leak that was spraying the crawl space liner.

I took a few digital pictures of the leak and repaired it myself. I then called the Water Department and they sent me a Plumbers Affidavit. I filled it out, included my pictures, and a few weeks later I had a credit that paid my monthly bill the next 4 months.

All it took was a few pictures and a phone call to help save some money.

You can get reimbursed in other ways, such as at work or with an organization you serve in. If you use your personal cell phone for work calls often, ask your boss if they would consider reimbursing you or giving you a cell phone allowance. If you help in an organization with supplies or food, just ask if they will reimburse you.

You have to make sure you keep your receipts and all you have to do is ask. The worse thing they could say is no, but in many cases they will understand and support your request.

14. Ask For A Corporate Discount

One of the ways of saving money often overlooked is the discounts we get by working for a certain employer. This is such an easy one and all you have to do is ask. Here is a list of some places that I have had experience with in offering corporate discounts:

- Cell phone carriers
- Cable company
- Restaurants
- Auto mechanics / Tire stores
- Gym memberships
- Hotels
- Auto companies (if you work in the auto industry)

If you are married and the business does not offer a discount for your employer, ask about your spouse's employer. It is also helpful to ask your HR department what businesses they are aligned with to gain employee savings.

15. Don't Sign Up and Settle

We have all signed up for various services and forget about them. We assume the price is set from the day of service, but that may not always be the case. The services I am talking about could be with your cable television provider, utility provider, a bank, or another monthly billed service.

Let's use cable television for example. When you signed up you chose a specific programming package. As time goes by you realize you do not watch many of the channels you are paying for. Once you realize this, call your provider and ask for a lower cost option. If you use different companies for phone, cable, and internet see if any of the companies offer a bundled savings discount.

Many providers run promotions or offer programs to help you save. Call them and ask if they have any lower cost options, any suggestions that could help save on your bill, or if they are offering any promotions. The key is to always evaluate that you are getting the best value after you have signed up for a service.

16. Save With Samples

I have a drawer full of soaps, shampoos, and lotions from various hotels I travel to. I usually pack any unused item from each trip (except shower caps). Saving these samples can prevent you from paying for them at your local store. Stores generally charge about $1 a piece. You can use these for future trips, camping, a guest bath, or as a backup when your normal item runs out to stretch those dollars.

Another way to get samples is directly from manufacturers. Look at who makes your favorite products and see if they offer samples. If you want to try something new, check out the manufacturer's website to see if you can get a sample first before you potentially waste your money. If they do not have anything on their site, send them an e-mail asking if they would provide you with a sample.

If you prefer not to use the samples you accumulate I would encourage you to donate them to a local shelter or food pantry. I took a full container of trial size soaps, shampoos, and toothpastes to a shelter and they were so appreciative. It is a simple way we can help others.

17. Smart Phone Savings

With smart phones today there are many ways through its apps, technology, and its mobility that can help you land savings. I will highlight the ways my phone has proven its investment and helped me become a better consumer. Just try searching your app store for "coupons" and you will find some that display nearby savings depending on your location.

A favorite app of mine is Key Ring™. It allows you to store all your loyalty cards on it which saves space in your purse or wallet. It also shows you any savings at those stores.

It is amazing how smart phones have been able to turn into products we use. You can turn it into a flashlight, use it to verify if something is level, or even tune a guitar with it. There are three products I want to highlight that a smart phone can save you a lot of money.

Weather Alert App - If you do not have a weather radio yet, downloading a weather alert app could save you money and your life. Many television stations provide apps you can use, so you can be informed of weather alerts in your area.

Camera – Last year on vacation our digital camera accidentally fell in the pool. We delayed buying a new camera almost one year by using our phone camera instead. Smart phone cameras have become so much better in quality over the past couple years. They can help delay or prevent the expense of buying a new digital camera.

GPS - Before buying a GPS or paying to update your car's GPS software consider using your smart phone's free navigational apps that work just as effectively. By using a phone app you get the benefit of finding directions even outside of your car, such as walking downtown in a big city, or discussing directions with a friend at lunch.

In addition to the added flexibility, you do not have to worry about having to update the software. With GPS devices you need to update the software every so often to keep up with new roads, new businesses, and changing phone numbers. Sometimes those updates are free or there is a fee. Either way you have the hassle factor. Updating the GPS software in your car can cost up to $250. You have now created a new meaning of GPS that stands for Good Practical Savings.

Another way to save money with your smart phone is to shop online while you are in a brick-and-mortar store. You are probably wondering how this is possible. Initially, one would think that you shop at one or the other, not both simultaneously. When we are at a store it is easy to buy something because of convenience. On items typically over $30 that I am in no rush for I may do a quick search on my phone to see if I can get cheaper. There are barcode scanner apps too that help do price comparing. Make sure you take into consideration shipping costs. It really depends on the item, but generally I will delay an in-store purchase to buy on the internet if I can save at least $10 or more.

18. Monitor A Price After Purchase

We all like to purchase something at its lowest price. I have waited around for weeks hoping an item will go on sale. Did you know many stores allow you up to 30 days to notify them after purchase if the item you bought is a lower price?

I purchased a lawn tractor and sure enough the price lowered the week after I bought it. I took my receipt in, showed them the ad, and it saved me about $90. I also bought a television stand and just three days after I got it delivered I saw an ad where it was at a lower price. I called the store to verify it was the same product number and it was. They made the price adjustment over the phone and I did not have to come to the store. Just looking at the ad and making a phone call saved me $77.

This happens a lot with common sale items such as electronics, appliances, and furniture. Keep your receipt and just check your weekly ads, at the store, online store, or make a quick call. This idea can gain you big savings and all you have to do is a little follow up.

19. Share With Your Neighbor

How good of a neighbor are you? I am careful with this idea because it can lead to a nagging neighbor who always wants to borrow something from you, but it can also lead to saving money for you. It is impossible, and impractical to have every tool or piece of equipment needed for your home. Having a good, trusting relationship with your neighbors can help keep you from buying expensive tools that you will only use a few times in your life.

In the first subdivision my wife and I lived, people were very good at caring for their lawns. Each fall, one of the neighbors would go around and gauge interest in those wanting to share in the cost of renting a lawn aerator. A few homes would agree and it would help split the cost to each home to 1/5, plus you would not have to go pick it up. It was a convenient way to save money with neighbors joining together.

Here are some recommended things for sharing. These are basically pricey categories that may not be worth the investment for that seldom use:

- Various power tools
- Car maintenance tools
- Extension Ladder
- Air Compressor
- Lawn Equipment
- Sports Equipment

Do not be afraid to ask a neighbor if they have an item you can use. Make sure you ask them how to use the borrowed item so you do not break it or get hurt. Plus read the instructions of the item. Also, make sure you return the item borrowed quickly. You do not want them to keep your item for months. Lastly, put your name on your items, so they do not get mixed up or forgotten.

20. Barter Like The Old Days

Building off the sharing with your neighbor concept, put your gifted skills to work for you. Maybe you like to mow yards and you have a computer problem at home. Instead of hiring a computer technician, find that computer savvy friend and offer to mow their yard in return for fixing your computer.

Offer to help someone play guitar, so you can learn how to golf. Help someone with some painting if they could fix your car. Teach someone how to cook and they can teach you how to speak Spanish.

The opportunities to trade skills are limitless! Understand what you can offer and keep note of what skills certain friends have. This idea not only helps build relationships, but can help you save money as well.

21. Share Your Feedback

We work hard for our money and we expect the things we buy to meet our needs. Too often we just assume it is not under warranty, not worth the hassle of contacting the manufacturer, or we are too impatient and we go out and buy the replacement.

I am not advocating that you become a complainer to get free stuff, but simply share your feedback with companies when you are genuinely disappointed. On the flip side, if you are very pleased with a product, share your glowing review with the company as well.

Manufacturers want to hear your feedback good and bad, especially concerns you have. This is how they can improve the quality of their product. Do not assume you have to return an item at the store you bought it or that you still have to have your receipt. Look up the manufacturers contact info and reach out to them directly.

CHOICES THAT SAVE

22. Pay in Advance

If you own a business or work in a business setting, you know how important cash flow is. It is very hard to tie up your money, but for the right deal it could be worth paying in advance. This really applies to a cost you incur every month. I have seen lawn care companies give a 5-10% discount if you pay a season in advance versus paying monthly. Subscription services are other examples where you can save by buying a year or more at a time.

If you buy magazines periodically, it is probably a good idea to just buy a subscription up front. However not buying magazines is a quicker way to save. You may be able to get that information online anyways.

Buying gifts in advance is another way to save. Throughout the year, if I find a good deal on something that I know someone would like for their birthday or Christmas I go ahead and get it. Just try not to forget you bought it when that occasion arrives.

23. Drink Water When Dining Out

What a great way to save money and dine healthier. Restaurants charge about $2.00 these days for having a soft drink with your meal. My dad and I went to Las Vegas and at one nationally known restaurant chain the soft drink cost $4.29.

If you are like our family, we eat out a few times a week. All you have to do is substitute water for the soft drink each time. If we substituted for our family of 4 on 3 meals during a week and a drink cost $2.00 that would equate to a savings of $1,248 a year. Just substitute water half the time and you would still save $624 per year.

It is difficult to go cold turkey on sodas, so buy yourself a $4.00 12-pack for home. You can still get your craving in at home for about $.33 per can or less. Do not forget the health benefits of drinking more water per day.

24. Morning Drink Alternatives

There are so many people who buy premium coffee or a soda every morning. Choosing an alternative is an easy way to save money instantly. A $3 cup of coffee 5 days a week equates to $780 a year. A $1 soft drink 5 days a week equates to $260.

Yes premium coffee or soda may taste good, but consider other alternatives. First, starting with coffee, you could brew your own. You can buy premium blends at the store or check out the new home brewing systems. Another alternative is to drink company supplied coffee. You can add flavored creamer to enhance the taste. With soda consider drinking water. You can buy a case of 24 bottled waters for the price of about 3 soft drinks.

You do not have to cut your coffee or soda out completely, but purchase them less frequently. If you buy a soda every weekday, substituting another option one day a week will save you over $50 a year or choosing an alternative over coffee would save over $150 a year.

25. The Home Workout

Staying healthy is so important. When your body is healthy you are reducing the chance of medical bills and enjoying a happier life. With that said, working out is one way to obtain a healthy body.

First consult your physician, develop a plan of exercise routines you want to do, and then purchase the necessary equipment. This will require money up front, but the payoff is huge!

Let's determine the Return on Investment:

- Cost of purchasing home gym equipment: $1,000
- Gym fee to join: $50 (some go as high as $200)
- Monthly gym membership fee average: $40

Return on investment (ROI) = approximately 2 years.

On the home equipment purchase, I went with a basic treadmill and weight system (universal). I actually spent less than $1,000 for both. Shop around to find the best value for your exercise needs.

I will admit that is a stretch for me to wait 2 years for pay off. But if you assume you use that equipment for an additional 5 years, you have just saved $2,400.

Bonus: Do not forget all the time you just put back into your schedule by not having to travel to the gym. You will save gas money and not have to wait for a machine to free up. Go ahead, turn on some tunes, workout safely, and start turning those weights into dollars.

26. Donate

Before you throw those old clothes, toys, or household items in the trash, see if you can help extend their life by donating to a non-for-profit organization. Whenever we have items left over from a garage sale we drop off our remaining items at one of these great organizations. Make sure the donated items are in good condition.

When you drop your items off ask for a receipt. By the time tax season rolls around, you could claim your charitable contribution. Make sure to review this with an accounting professional for guidelines on how much can be applied and how you could benefit. Be honest with your giving. This is a commonly overlooked tax benefit, which could help you save and help others save with your generosity.

27. Newspapers

Do you get a daily newspaper? Do the papers ever stack up for a few days and when you finally get a chance to read them you realize its old news? That was the case for me and soon I was staring at wasted dollars stacking up with the next stop destination: recycling bin.

Check with your newspaper provider and see if there is a Sunday only subscription. This can save you over a hundred dollars a year. You want to continue to get the Sunday paper because of its valuable advertisements and coupons.

Many newspapers now provide the same printed stories online. Sometimes online stories may be posted hours later and this allows you to see the story before it is printed the next day.

28. Visit the Library

When was the last time you visited the library? For most people it has been a long time. Do not take for granted the resources your local library has to offer. The library is a great source to gain knowledge and save money. Go take advantage of your tax dollars at work!

- Music & Movies – Most libraries have an offering, although limited, of CDs or DVDs that you can borrow. Before you buy them, check it out from the library first to see if you like it. Also, instead of renting a movie, opt to borrow one from the library instead.

- How-to Guides – if you want to learn how to do home or auto repairs, build a project, or learn a new skill the library has many books to help.

- E-books – More libraries are now offering free e-books you can download to an e-reader.

- Computer access – if you cannot afford a computer or yours breaks down, the library is a good backup source.

29. Fuel Savings

For many of us buying fuel for our cars is one of our biggest monthly expenses. With the fluctuations in fuel prices it makes it hard to budget and the cost continues to rise. Here are a few ways I try to reduce my cost at the pump:

Gas Buddy™ - One of my favorite smart phone apps is the Gas Buddy™ app (also can use: www.gasbuddy.com). Most of us either get gas at the first place you see or you drive around forever spending more money looking for cheaper gas than the few cents savings you eventually find. The Gas Buddy™ app is so helpful. It shows me all the prices of gas near me and which one is the cheapest. This allows me to save time and money.

Air Filter – make sure you or someone checks the cleanliness of your air filter periodically. Ensuring you have a clean filter helps increase your engines performance and improve gas mileage.

Tire Pressure – It is always a safe idea to adhere to your cars tire pressure guidelines. Making sure you have the right tire pressure can also help with your mileage. Per www.fueleconomy.gov, you can improve your gas mileage by 3.3% by keeping your tires at their proper pressure.

Discount Clubs – These mega stores require a fee to join, but the savings in gas alone could be worth it. In the city we recently moved from the savings was about $0.10 per gallon. In the city we moved to it has been up to $0.30 per gallon less expensive. That is about a $5 savings per each fill up with my truck.

30. Greeting Card Alternatives

On special occasions it is nice to give someone a card to show your love, appreciation, concern, or other feeling of emotion. Cards are funny and well written, but they are also pricey. The price of cards has also gone up substantially over the recent years.

Let's do a quick exercise in about how many cards one could buy during one year. Birthday, Valentine's Day, Anniversary, Thank You, Get Well/Sympathy, Graduation, New Baby, Easter, Christmas......you could easily buy 6-10 cards per year. At $4 a pop, plus time to go pick them out, you have spent $24-$40 in cards that many will end up in a trash can.

Saving suggestions:

- If you have children, let them make the cards. These become great keepsakes and are more meaningful to the recipient.

- Unleash your inner-child by making a card yourself

- Send an electronic card or e-mail

- Buy a box of assorted greeting cards

I do not suggest eliminating buying cards completely, but consider these few alternatives from time to time. By introducing these options on occasion you can save $15-$25 per year.

31. Pay Cash

You are probably wondering how paying with cash can save money. Well, actually it works. When places have to use a credit card to process your payment they incur processing fees. Many places encourage cash because they do not have to pay the processing fee or worry about a questionable check.

Paying by cash and earning a savings is normally successful when you are paying for service related items. The best example, I can give you is when you are having someone work on a project for you. It could be adding a patio, building something, painting, and even buying a car.

Once you have come to an agreement on the cost of a particular service ask that company what kind of discount you would get if you paid cash. I say my success rate on this is about 30% of the time. You can save from 1% and I have seen as high as a 10% discount on your bill. Make sure you still get a receipt. You were going to pay the same amount either way, so ask the question, pony up the cash, and save away.

32. Avoid Credit Card Interest

When I was in 5th grade I got my first credit card at a mall department store.   You had your choice of $100 or $200 limit and of course parents had to co-sign.   Since I wanted this new stereo that was over $100, I got the $200 limit. At that time my parents had two reasons to let me have a credit card.   The first reason was to start building my credit rating in case I wanted to take a loan out for a car or for college. The second reason was to teach me responsibility and the importance of not paying interest.   I learned that lesson on the first bill!

When my first bill arrived my parents told me to only pay part of it.   I had saved up all my allowance and birthday money to pay it all off, but they said "We want to teach you a simple lesson."   I paid a portion and listened happily to my new tunes. Next month the bill came in and what did I see?   INTEREST!   I thought that was crazy and I realized at that young age it was like giving your money away. From that day forward I have never paid one cent of interest on a credit card. I pay off every bill in full and on time.

Your credit rating is so important and by not paying interest you are allowing yourself to qualify for a car loan or a mortgage at a much better interest rate. The less interest you pay on those the more money you save.

Do what you can to pay off credit card bills in full and on time, so you avoid giving money away to interest.

33. Automatic Payment Deductions

Over the past seven years, we have moved into a new house twice. With declining interest rates we refinanced twice to shorten our mortgage timeframe and lower the interest rate. Each time we completed one of these big financial decisions we took advantage of the banks Automatic Mortgage Deduction Discount. We saved 0.25% on our interest rate. It depends on the home price and current interest rate, but if we assume your home is $100,000, interest is 4.5%, and you have a 30-year mortgage, the savings per month is about $17 or $200 a year.

A new trend with banks is that they want you to enroll in automatic payment programs. One of our banks offered us an incentive to sign up monthly bills to be automatically paid by our bank account. It applied to cable providers, water department, insurance company, utilities, newspaper, and others. They were offering 1,000 points per account setup and a maximum of 5,000 points. The 5,000 points equated to a $25 gift card through their rewards program. Ask your bank if they offer any incentive for setting up automatic payments with your service providers.

34. Loan Refinancing

When you have a loan, periodically monitor the interest rates. You can check with bankrate.com or directly with your bank. As I mentioned before, we refinanced our mortgage twice and in each time we were able to shorten the mortgage timeframe and obtain a lower interest rate. The first refinance we went from a 30-year loan to a 20-year loan. In the second home we refinanced from a 30-year loan to a 15-year loan. In both cases, we also got interest rates at about 1.25% lower than where we stood at the 30-year mortgage rate.

When refinancing there are upfront closing costs associated with this. You need to make sure you have the savings to be able to do it. I did a quick break-even analysis in both of my refinances and in one case it was 7 months and in the other it was 11 months. To me these were smart moves plus it shortened the loan timeframe allowing me to pay hundreds more per month on the principal. Refinancing, when done correctly, can help you save thousands of dollars over a several year period.

35. Replace Gifts With Gift Cards

I am a very hard person to buy for. I can honestly say that I feel very blessed and have what I need. However, my lack of ideas for others makes it very difficult for them to buy me something for Christmas. I have started to tell them now that I can always use a gift card at one of my favorite stores. Next time someone asks you for a gift idea, suggest a gift card.

- Make sure you give them store ideas you like
- Make sure you use up the entire card. Keep it in front of you so you do not forget it.
- Be practical with it and try to use part of it to offset a needed expense, but also buy something fun for yourself that you would normally not treat yourself to.

When buying restaurant gift cards for others you should search for restaurants that offer a bonus. You will see these bonuses around the holidays and they typically average about $10 for every $50 you spend. If you buy $100 worth, you could earn $20 back to help pay for dinner.

36. Reduce Your Utility Bills

There are many sources today that share ways to reduce your utility bills. I want to highlight a few I have incorporated into my home.

- Insulate receptacles. Did you realize that your receptacles inside your home along exterior walls can let in air? Go to a home improvement store and ask for these inexpensive, easy to install insulators.

- Clean out your clothes dryer vent. Our dryer was taking twice as long to dry clothes. I thought it was because it was 14 years old. My dad noticed the outside vent was clogged and that was the reason.

- Caulk your windows where air is getting in and out.

- Close off crawl space vents in the winter and open them in the summer.

- Close off draft points during the winter months by putting safe draft blockers at bottom of exterior doors.

- Add a solid screen door to help block air as well

- Programmable thermostats. A properly set programmable thermostat can save a household up to $180 per year, per www.energystar.gov. Check with your utility company for rebates. I got a $20 rebate for each programmable thermostat I installed.

- Visit your utility provider's website for ideas. When I went to our utility provider's site I saw where I could get 15 free CFL (low watt) bulbs. I took advantage of that savings.

- Sign up for a Home Energy Assessment. Many utility providers offer this and it takes about one hour. At the end of my assessment I received a box of CFL bulbs, sink aerators, and new shower heads. I would estimate that box was worth almost $100.

- Make sure you check with your Utility Provider, State, or Accountant on any tax credits or rebates you may qualify for with any home energy efficient products you purchase.

PROMOTIONS & PROGRAMS

37. Loyalty / Reward Cards

This is one of the easiest ways to save money and gain special perks, but it can take some time until you receive your reward. When I used to travel a lot I signed up for the rewards card at every hotel and airline I used. Over time you accumulate so many points that before you know it you have enough for a free airline ticket or a free hotel stay.

Reward cards are typically known in the airline and hotel industries, but many places now offer them. From coffee shops to electronics stores, gas stations to pharmacies, and more. More stores now are giving you instant coupons or bonuses, such as gift cards or free merchandise.

Many people hesitate to sign up because they do not want to mess with the time and hassle of signing up or they do not want to receive junk mail. It is simple and worth it! You do not have to stress out about keeping all your cards in order. Use the Key Ring™ app or many places can just pull your name up in the system and apply your account to your purchase.

38. Promotional Items

One of the ways companies get you to buy their products is by enticing us with promotional items. You may get an item for free at an event or you get the item by purchasing a product. One area I have been able to benefit from greatly in is with cologne shopping. Duffel/gym bags are the common giveaways. I have not purchased a gym bag in over 10 years.

If you like a cologne that does not have a promotional giveaway or you do not like what they are offering negotiate with the clerk. Most of the time they can substitute with another item you prefer or they can give you multiple items. Do not be surprised if you luck into getting multiple promotional items with your purchase.

Another great way to score promotional goodies is at trade shows or business expos. You can get shirts, flash drives, bags, notebooks, pens, water bottles and more. Plus, you get chances to win some nice prizes. You can use that free shirt around the house, use those bags at home or travel, and you can never have too many office supplies. I recommend only attending shows if they are of no or minimal expense to you.

Promotional giveaways come in a wide range of ways. Do not be shy when it comes to these giveaways. Companies want to give away these items to gain marketing exposure, so take advantage of it. If you do not like the promotional item accompanying a purchase, ask if there is a substitute. If you do like the item, ask if they will give you an extra one or two and you will have a good chance that they will give you an extra item for free.

39.   Free Money For College

This idea will not pay for your child's entire college tuition, but it is free money and helps with expenses. The most popular company is Upromise®. They have an agreement with hundreds of retailers we commonly shop at. Account setup is easy and free.

On the Upromise® website there is links to all the retailers making it a nice, consolidated way to shop multiple places quickly. It helps if you want to see store choices for a certain product category and also helps if you want to do quick comparison shopping. The site will show you what the savings amount is you will receive that will be put into your child's Upromise® account for college use.

The real hidden value of using the Upromise® site is they regularly provide you current coupon codes being honored at the retailer's site which will net you immediate savings on top of the college savings. I keep Upromise® as a favorite on my toolbar and before I buy anything I look there for coupon codes.

40. Multi-Benefit Memberships

One of the things our family loves to do is go to the zoo. It is a wonderful way to spend family time together, get exercise, and enjoy animals from all over the world. We discovered that at our city's zoo we could get an annual family membership for the price of about two visits. This allows unlimited admission for the family all year long and discounts for food and souvenirs.

What is also great is the zoo is part of a national association of zoos and aquariums. You can use your card for discounts at other zoos and aquariums. We were able to get into more expensive zoos in bigger cities for free or ½ off! The cost of a single-day admission to one of those zoos was almost the equivalent to our annual membership fee. Our small investment paid for itself over and over and saved us hundreds of dollars.

We have also bought memberships at other local attractions such as the aquarium and a train museum. In each case the break-even was about two visits. We knew we would attend more than that throughout the year, so it became a no brainer. We get enjoyment out of these visits, some are educational, we get good exercise each time, and we are able to create great memories.

GO START SAVING

By now I hope I have given you a few new ideas to think about and incorporate into your money saving game plan. As I mentioned at the beginning of the book, not all ideas will apply and not all will be successful. However, you can be successful in many of these ideas. The key takeaway is; change your mindset in how you approach buying things and managing your expenses and you will be surprised at how much you can save.

As I took a leap of faith in sharing this book with you, I knew in my heart that everyone works so hard and yet this economy is getting more challenging. We have to be smarter consumers. My attempt in this book is just to share with you a collection of ideas to help you. I did not set out on this journey to make a bunch of money. I told my wife when I started composing this book that I just wanted to help people. I hope I have been successful in my goal to help you by giving you ways to save your hard earned money.

Some final tips:

- Research the product – Make sure it offers everything you want for the price you are willing to spend.

- Know your options – Invest a little time to shop around. Unless there is a great deal at the store, see if you can find it cheaper online.

- Always think like a money saver – Negotiate when you can and look for ways to save on the purchase. Think outside the box.

- Trust in yourself that you can be a savvy consumer.

- Take saving money seriously. Do not let this be a flavor of the month approach. Let this be a Game Changer in your life!

Money Saving

Game Plan

Here is a list of all the strategies I just shared with you to help guide and encourage you. Using your list:

1. Highlight the tips and strategies that apply to you today or will in the near future.

2. Identify five of them to focus on during the next week. Pick ones you know you will have an opportunity to save on, plus with a high probability of success. This will create momentum without getting overwhelmed, and help you start building the money saving mindset foundation.

3. Using your list, jot down next to those five ideas all the different ways you think you can achieve savings.

4. Once you have completed this strategizing exercise, it is now time to start saving. Keep reviewing the ideas and keep generating more how's and when's to save.

5. After you have finished your first week, make a note of what worked and what did not. Also, track your savings on the list.

6. Next, pick a new set of ideas you want to tackle and start saving more.

This game plan is just a simple tool to help you prioritize which ideas apply to you (hopefully most) and which ones you want to target first. Brainstorm ways you could generate savings with each idea, identify which ones are successful or not, and track your estimated savings so you can see how well you have done in building your Money Saving Mindset.

You can also find this list on my website:

www.amoneysavingmindset.com

	IDEAS TO ACHIEVE THIS GOAL	SUCCESSFUL (Y/N)	ESTIMATED SAVINGS
1. ONLINE SHOPPING			
2. LEVERAGE THE COMPETITION			
3. IN-STORE COUPONS			
4. DO YOUR RESEARCH			
5. BUYING CLOTHES			
6. OFF SEASON VALUES			
7. DOLLAR STORE VALUES			
8. REVIEW YOUR RECEIPTS			
9. BUYING A USED CAR			
10. NEGOTIATE			

	IDEAS TO ACHIEVE THIS GOAL	SUCCESSFUL (Y/N)	ESTIMATED SAVINGS
11. REUSE / REPURPOSE			
12. A FRESH COAT OF SAVINGS			
13. GET REIMBURSED			
14. ASK FOR A CORPORATE DISCOUNT			
15. DON'T SIGN UP AND SETTLE			
16. SAVE WITH SAMPLES			
17. SMART PHONE SAVINGS			
18. MONITOR PRICE AFTER PURCHASE			
19. SHARE WITH YOUR NEIGHBOR			
20. BARTER LIKE THE OLD DAYS			

	IDEAS TO ACHIEVE THIS GOAL	SUCCESSFUL (Y/N)	ESTIMATED SAVINGS
21. SHARE YOUR FEEDBACK			
22. PAY IN ADVANCE			
23. DRINK WATER WHEN DINING OUT			
24. MORNING DRINK ALTERNATIVES			
25. THE HOME WORKOUT			
26. DONATE			
27. NEWSPAPERS			
28. VISIT THE LIBRARY			
29. FUEL SAVINGS			
30. GREETING CARD ALTERNATIVES			

	IDEAS TO ACHIEVE THIS GOAL	SUCCESSFUL (Y/N)	ESTIMATED SAVINGS
31. PAY CASH			
32. AVOID CREDIT CARD INTEREST			
33. AUTOMATIC PAYMENT DEDUCTIONS			
34. LOAN REFINANCING			
35. REPLACE GIFTS WITH GIFT CARDS			
36. REDUCE YOUR UTILITY BILLS			
37. LOYALTY / REWARD CARDS			
38. PROMOTIONAL ITEMS			
39. FREE MONEY FOR COLLEGE			
40. MULTI-BENEFIT MEMBERSHIPS			

Jesus looked at them and said,

"With man this is impossible, but with God all things are possible."

- Matthew 19:26 (New International Version®)

My Prayer for You

Moving forward my prayer for you is that you will continue to gain wisdom as a consumer. I pray that you will find ways to save money and live a financially responsible life. While those things are important, I pray that more importantly you realize that the ultimate savings is not with money, but with the savings (treasures in heaven) you get from being a faithful follower of Jesus Christ.

I put my trust in Jesus Christ, March 2003, thanks to a persistent and God-loving wife. It changed my life in an awesome way. If you have never invited Christ into your heart, all it takes is a heartfelt prayer like this:

"Dear Heavenly Father, I know I am a sinner. Please forgive me of my sins. I believe you sent Jesus Christ down to this earth to live a sinless life. He made the ultimate sacrifice by dying on the cross and rose from the dead, all so we could be forgiven of our sins. From this day forward, I accept Jesus Christ as my personal Lord and Savior."

If you said this prayer, you have made the best decision in your life. Please reach out to a local pastor and they will guide you on the next steps of your new Christian life.

About the Author

Derek Polen grew up in a small Indiana town, raised in a blue-collar household, and by cost-conscious parents. A lifelong learner, Derek has various business degrees, including an MBA. Derek has also completed professional development and continuing education courses from Duke, Harvard, Indiana University, M.I.T., and Northwestern. His professional experience includes roles in Product Management and Supply Chain Management.

When he is not going on adventures with his family, he likes investing in the stock market, watching old movies, or following his favorite sports teams. Derek is a follower of Jesus Christ and forever thankful to his personal Savior.

Check out:

www.amoneysavingmindset.com